PYTHON PROGRAMMING

BEGINNERS GUIDE TO LEARN PYTHON PROGRAMMING AND ANALYSIS. UNLOCK YOUR POTENTIAL AND DEVELOP YOUR PROJECT IN FEW DAYS

AUTHOR: NICK LESSON

Table of Contents

Introduction

Python refers to an interpreting and scripting language, which is object-oriented. It falls under the category of high-level programming languages and exhibits dynamic semantics. Python has high level inbuilt data structures as well as dynamic typing and binding, making it a suitable fit for Rapid Application Development. It can also be used as a glue or scripting language for joining together already existing components. Owing to its syntax, which is relatively simple and easy to learn, Python emphasizes readability, thus curbing the cost of maintaining the program. Python also supports packages and modules which foster reusing codes and modularizing the program.

How is Python Used?

Python is a programming language that can be used for many purposes. However, most important of all, Python is an interpreted language, meaning that during run-time, its written code isn't converted into a format that is readable by the computer. Whereas, many programming languages require this translation to be done before the program can be run. Programming languages with such qualities were known as scripting languages in the past because they were used to carry out trivial tasks. Albeit, this nomenclature changed as a result of Python. The reason is that it is commonplace for broad applications to be written almost exclusively in Python in contemporary times.

The application of Python can be used in the following ways:

1. In working with Files

2. In programming CGI for Web Applications

3. In reading from and Writing to PostgreSQL

4. In building RSS Readers

5. In reading from and writing to MySQL

6. In creating Calendars in HTML

How Can Python Help Me?

You've learned a little about what Python is, but how can learning Python help you in your everyday life? One of the ways is that Python can actually help you get a job or even excel at your current job.

Python can be used to help with certain applications that you may be using in your job. For example, if you work for a software company, you may use Python for text processing. Text processing is going to help you log in files to your database so that you can easily access them and know what you need to do when you need to do it.

Python will also help you when it comes to jobs such as web design and even programming, which is a given. With the many functions of Python, you can use it for virtually any job that you could ever want. The only thing

z

is that you will need to learn all of the different modules that Python has to offer in order to use Python for the specification of your job.

Even if your job does not use Python, you may be able to bring it into the workplace so that you can make things easier on yourself and your co-workers. Doing this will demonstrate initiative to your boss and may even earn you a promotion.

How to Learn Python

Figure Out a Reason for Learning Python

In learning Python programming, the primary step to take is figuring out the "why" element. To learn Python and target it towards fulfilling your needs, you have to decipher why exactly you want to learn it. This process is vital in helping you decipher what you would get out of the process and could be your motivation in the long run. It is also helpful in identifying the best way to get started as well as the other necessary skills required for the process.

In finding your 'why,' ponder on the following:

Why Python?

In learning to code, it is advisable to have a goal in sight during the learning process. Determining the level of skill you want to attain and how you hope to use that skill are vital factors to ponder on in picking a language. Pondering on these should help you decipher if Python is the right programming language for you. Also, you would be able to narrow down your choice of courses to reach your goals. Python, in itself, has its limits, so be sure it is the language that satisfies your needs and goals.

What Plans Have You Got for Learning Python?

If your reason for learning Python is to further a career in programming, you have to take to mind the skills necessary to succeed in your chosen field. For instance, if you want to enter the field of developing back-end web applications using Python, you would have to master skills in web development and framework.

How Much Time Can You Put into the Learning Process?

Deciphering how much time you can commit to the learning process is an essential factor to consider. The reason is that it is advisable not to take on more responsibilities than one can handle. It is possible to enroll in any course offering Python but making time out to commit to it is critical. If you have a limited amount of time to learn Python, your commitment to the learning process would be limited. Thus, you wouldn't be able to partake in physical classes that clash with your schedule. In this case, an online course is your best bet.

Chapter 1: Origin of Python

Python started as an idea back in 1989, when Guido van Rossum became aware of the shortcomings of the ABC language, mostly with extensibility. Rossum began to develop a new language, one that included all the great features that ABC had and some new features, like exception handling and extensibility. In 1994, the very first edition of Python was released, taking its system of modules from Modula-3, incorporating programming tools that were incredibly functional and being able to interact with Amoeba, an early operating system.

In 2000, Python 2.0 made its entrance into the programming world, a much-improved version with lots more improvisations, such as Unicode support and a garbage collector. Over the next 8 years, Python 2.0 was updated several times, and in December of 2008, Python 3.0 was released.

Backward compatibility was no longer possible with Python 3.0, meaning that you must either use 2.0 or 3.0, not both. Python 3.0 also gained a new design as a way of avoiding duplicative modules and constructs. However, it is still multi-paradigm, and it still offers developers all the options that a structured programming language offers, including functional programming, and it is still object oriented.

Today, Python comes in several different implementations, including IronPython, which is written for the Common Language Infrastructure in C#, Python, in the Java language and designed for Java Virtual Machine and PyPy, which was originally written in Rpython and then translated to C. However, by far the most popular implementation is CPython, a language that was developed by the Python Software Foundation. All of these will work on the language they are written in and can also interact with multiple other languages by using modules, most of which are free and open source. Python 3.4.2 was released in 2015 and offers significant improvements and new features, including better Unicode support.

Applications for Python

Python is used for many different applications, including:

- Desktop applications that are GUI-based

- Applications for graphic design and image processing

- Computational applications

- Scientific applications

- Games

- Web applications and web frameworks

- Business and enterprise applications

- Language development

- Operating systems

- Prototyping

How Python Compares to Other Languages

Owing to its popularity, Python is commonly brought under comparison with other interpreted languages, including, but not limited to the following; Smalltalk, Java, TCL, JavaScript, Perl, etcetera. There are also some comparisons made to Scheme, Common Lisp and C++. In comparing Python to these languages, the focus would be placed on issues regarding each language alone. Technically, the choice of any programming language depends on other apparent factors like training, cost, prior investment, availability, and sometimes even sentiments. Hence, this section is not an advantage comparison to prove what programming language is better than another.

Perl

Perl and Python share similarities in background; both of them coming from Unix scripting, which they have now outgrown. Another similarity exists in the features they both have. The only concise difference between Python and Perl is found in their philosophies. Perl places emphasis on the support of basic application-oriented tasks. For example, Perl has built-in regular expression, report generating features, and file scanning. Python, on the other hand, places more support on basic methods of programming like object-oriented programming and the design of data structure. Python further goes on to support programmers in creating codes with easy readability and maintainability by offering a notation that is elegant but not too cryptic. As a result, Python comes near Perl in this regard but seldom ever trumps the latter in its actual application domain. Albeit, Python possesses applicability, which is well over the niche Perl operates in.

Common Lisp and Scheme

Common Lisp and Scheme both share proximity with Python as a result of the dynamics of their semantics. However, they possess a distinct method of syntax, which makes any comparison somewhat of a debate. The argument is whether or not Lisp's lack of syntax is advantageous or disadvantageous. Keep in mind that Python possesses introspective capabilities that are akin to those seen in Lisp. Also, Python programs can create and execute fragments of programs on the go. In this debate, factors affecting the real world are decisive elements: Common Lisp is quite large, and the world of Scheme is a fragment of many different incompatible versions, whereas Python's implementation is both compact, single, and free.

Java

It is a general belief that python programs run somewhat slower than programs written in Java. However, they are developed much faster than Java's. In terms of length, Python programs are usually up to 3 to 5 times shorter than their equivalents in Java. This difference is primarily because of Python's in-built features such as dynamic typing and high-level data types. For instance, a programmer would have no hassle declaring the types of variables or arguments with Python, and the dictionary types and robust polymorphic list found in Python, for which a productive syntactic support system is built into the language, is hardly ever out of use in any python program.

As a result of the run-time typing, Java's run time works significantly less hard than Python's. For instance, in the evaluation of the expression x+y, Python has first to observe both objects (x and y) to decipher their type, which at compile time is yet unknown. It then proceeds to invoke the proper addition operation, which could turn out to be an overloaded method defined by the user. Conversely, Java is capable of performing a valid floating-point or integer addition but needs the variables x and y to be declared and would not allow the + operator to be overloaded in cases of user-defined classes. In this vein, Python seems better suited for the role of a "glue" language, while Java can be better used as a low-level implementation language. Different components can be developed in Java and joined to form python applications.

Conversely, Python can be used in prototyping components until their designs can be "hardened" in a Java implementation. To foster such a development, a python implementation coded in Java is currently being developed and would allow the calling of python codes from Java and vice versa. In doing this, Python's source code would be converted to Java bytecode by using a run-time library as support for the dynamic semantics of Python.

Smalltalk

The only arguable difference between Smalltalk and Python is that the latter has a more "mainstream" syntax that lends it an edge in programmer training. Dynamic typing and binding, and the fact that everything on Python being an object makes Python very much akin to Smalltalk. Albeit, Python differentiates built-in object types from user-defined classes and does not support inheritance from built-in types at the moment. The standard library of collection data in Smalltalk is better refined, while Python's library is equipped with more facilities focused on treating issues regarding the Internet and WWW realities like FTP, HTML, and email. Another distinction is evident in their different philosophies.

Python has a unique view of the development environment as well as the distribution of code. In cases where Smalltalk typically inserts a monolithic "system image," which involves both the user's program and the environment, Python saves both the standard modules and the user modules in separate files capable of being distributed or rearranged outside the system. A consequence of this is that a python program has several options for attaching a GUI (Graphical User Interface) because there is no in-built GUI in the system.

JavaScript

The "object-based" subset of Python is roughly equivalent to JavaScript. Unlike Java, Python supports a programming style that employs simple variables and functions without indulging in class definitions - a feature quite akin to JavaScript. Moreover, frankly, that is all there is to JavaScript. Python, however, supports the writing of much bigger programs and a better system of reusing codes via an actual object-oriented programming style, where inheritance and classes play vital roles.

C++

C++ contains most of the features discussed in Java, only with slight additions. While python codes are usually shorter than Java codes by up to 3 to 5 times, they are relatively 5 to 10 times shorter than their equivalents in C++. Evidence from anecdotes suggests that a single python programmer can complete what two C++ programmers won't finish in a year, in two months. Python serves as a glue language in the combination of components coded in C++.

Tcl

Similar to Python, Tcl can serve as a language for application extension and an individual programming language in its own right. Albeit, Tcl usually saves its data as strings, meaning that its data structures are weak, and as a result, would process codes way slower than Python. Besides this, Tcl is lacking in features necessary for writing big programs like modular namespaces. Hence, while a common extensive application running on Tcl typically contains extensions coded in C++ or C, which are particular to the application, its equivalent application in Python can be coded in pure Python. Moreover, the development of pure Python is a much more comfortable and quicker process than writing and debugging a C++ or C component.

It is a widespread belief that the only redeeming quality of Tcl lies in its Tk toolkit. Python adopted a similar interface to Tk for its traditional GUI component library. In addressing the problems of speed, Tcl 8.0 provides a bytecode compiler fitted with a ranged data type support system, mad additional namespaces. Albeit, regardless of these interventions, Tcl is still very much cumbersome a programming language.

PHP

PHP is gradually taking over as the official language of web development, displacing Perl in the process. Albeit, more than Perl or PHP, Python has better readability and can be quickly followed. The one disadvantage Perl has similar to PHP is the squirrely code. Also, coding programs that exceed the range of 50 to 100 lines become relatively more difficult as a result of the Perl and PHP's syntax. Conversely, Python is hardwired to be readable, down to the very fabric of the language. This readability makes it easier to extend and maintain programs written in Python. While PHP has begun to get more usage generally, it remains a programming language meant for the web regardless, designer to return web-readable information instead of handling system-level activities. This distinction is better exemplified by the fact that web servers coded in Python, which understand PHP, but it is impossible to develop a web server in PHP which understands Python. In conclusion, unlike Python, PHP is not object-oriented. This characteristic has a significant implication on the scalability, readability, and ease of maintenance of both programs.

Ruby

Python is often brought in comparison with Ruby. Both of them are interpreted high-level programming languages. Their codes are usually implemented in ways that understanding the details is not a requirement. They are just taken care of. Both Python and Ruby have their basis in object-oriented programming. Their method of implementing objects and classes makes for a more comfortable and better system of maintainability as well as code reuse. Both Python and Ruby are general-purpose languages and can be used in carrying out simple tasks like converting texts or more complicated activities like managing major financial data structures and programming and controlling robots. The significant distinction between the two languages, however, lies in their flexibility and readability. Owing to its nature of being object-oriented, Ruby codes have no errors in being squirrely as in PHP or Perl. Somewhat, it errs in being quite full and ends up as unreadable. Ruby tends to assume the intentions of the programmer. This feature begs the question many Ruby students often ask; "How does it know to do that?" In Python, the answer is straightforward; it is merely in its syntax. So, aside from being able to enforce indentation for readability, Python also enforces the transparency of information by assuming much less. Since it doesn't assume, Python makes for a smooth variation from the typical way of carrying out things when required while maintaining that the variation remains explicit in the code. By doing so, the programmer can do what is necessary while making sure that the code is sensible to those who read it afterward. Usually, after coding with Python, programmers find it quite challenging to switch to other programming languages.

Chapter 2: Benefits of Python Programming and Why Python is Better for Beginners?

Strengths of Python

1. **Simple to understand:** Python is quite easy to learn, and it doesn't have any intricate syntax and principles as followed with a different language. You are able to find out Python very easily in the event that you don't have some coding expertise. It is possible to say it's extremely user-friendly

2. **Free to use:** Python is free to use and accessible to get from its own official site. You may download Python by clicking the link provided here (download Python). The source code of Python can be obtained for the general public under GPL(general purpose license), from which you are able to download it, change it, exploit it, spread it. You're entirely free to do anything you would like to do using Python.

3. **Mobile:** portability is your primary strength of Python. User may run Python apps on several different platforms. Suppose you wrote an app in windows and you would like to run this app on Linux or Mac running system, you can readily run your apps on (windows, mac, Linux, raspberry pi, etc). You're able to state Python is a platform-independent programming language.

4. **Interpreted:** Python is a translated language, so it doesn't call for any sort of compiler to conduct the app. Python transforms its code to bytecode that gives immediate results. Python is translated signifies that the code is executed line by line that makes it simpler to debug.

5. **Extensible:** this is a really important strength of Python. To begin with, know the significance of extensible in Python, which it's developed in a means which lets the inclusion of new capacities and performance. It will allow you to port Python with libraries written in different languages. (mostly c or c++, however with c for a bridge you are able to predict different languages also that offer c ports.)

6. **Extensive libraries:** once you put in Python it has a high number of libraries that may be utilized for a particular function. You're able to download extra libraries in accordance with your requirement or job requirements. With the support of these libraries, so you do not need to compose the comprehensive code just apply these libraries and occupation performed using a few directions. Python offers libraries for internet browsers, picture manipulation, databases, email, and also for a number of different functions.

7. **Embeddable:** among the best features of Python is it is also embeddable. As an instance, you may embed YouTube video code to your HTML code. In the same way, it is possible to embed

Python code from another programming language such as c++. With this attribute, Python provides you the capacity to incorporate its code just like a script on your code in another language.

8. **Object-oriented:** Python could be applied as an object-oriented language where information structure and functions have been combined in one unit. Python supports both genders and procedure-oriented strategy from the evolution. The object-oriented approach addresses the interaction between the items, on the opposite hand, procedure-oriented strategy deals with purposes only.

9. **GUI programming:** Python provides lots of options to create a graphical user interface (GUI). Python delivered using a toolkit called TKINTER that's widely employed for GUI progress. By utilizing Python using TKINTER you're able to make GUI applications very quick and simple.

10. **Database connectivity:** Python supports each of the documents necessary for the maturation of different projects. Developers can select the very best suitable database to get their own projects. A few examples of databases that's encouraged by Python include mysql, postgresql, microsoft sql server, informix, interbase, oracle, and so forth.

Why Is Python Good for Beginners?

1. Less Coding

Almost all the tasks performed in Python requires less coding if the exact same task is completed in different languages. Python also offers a wonderful standard library service, and that means you don't need to hunt for any third-party libraries to get your task done. That is actually the reason that lots of men and women propose learning Python to novices.

2. Cheap

Python is free, so people, small businesses, or large organizations can leverage the free accessible tools to construct programs. Python is very popular and widely used and therefore provides you greater community service.

3. Python is for Everybody

Python code could run on any device if it's Linux, mac, or windows. Developers will need to learn unique languages for various tasks but using Python, you may professionally build web programs, play data analysis and machine learning and automate items, do internet scratching and build games, and strong visualizations. It's an all-rounder programming language.

Limitations

Each language has its limitations. Developers must understand these before beginning any new job. We've clarified all of the excellent things offered in Python, now the time will be to go over the flaws of Python.

1. **Speed**: Python is translated and implement code line by line that keeps it slower when compared with c++. If rate isn't the significant concern from the job, then you're advised to utilize Python.

2. **Bad for mobile development**: Python is the top terminology for server-side programming. However, as soon as we speak with respect to cellular development Python isn't too great. Here is the significant reason you will seldom find mobile applications developed with Python.

3. **Performance consumption**: Python has a very elastic structure for information. In case you've got a memory limit on your endeavor, then Python might not be a fantastic idea to utilize. Performance intake is on the other hand.

4. **Database access layer issues**: Python has problems with database access layers that limit it to utilize in a significant business.

5. **Run-time errors**: Python can provide you operate time errors that cause disappointment in the ending. Python is dynamically typed language, and also you also do not have to mention information type in applications that might wind up with run time errors.

Chapter 3: How to Code In Python: Basics of Python

Now that we have learned a bit more about the Python code and some of the things that you need to do in order to get this coding language set up on your computer, it is time to take a look at some of the different things that you can do with your code. We are going to start out with some of the basics and then will build on this when we get a bit further on in this guidebook to see some of the other things that we are able to do with this language. With this in mind, let's take a look at some of the basics that you need to know about any code in Python and all that you are going to be able to do with this coding language.

The Keywords in Python

The first part of the Python code that we are going to focus on is the Python keywords. These keywords are going to be reserved because they give the commands over to the compiler. You do not want to let these keywords show up in other parts of the code, and it is important to know that you are using them in the right part of the code.

Any time that you are using these keywords in the wrong manner or in the wrong part of the code, you are going to end up with some errors in place. These keywords are going to be there to tell your compiler what you wanted to happen, allowing it to know what it should do at the different parts of the code. They are really important to the code and will make sure that everything works in the proper manner and at the right times.

When you are taking a shot at another PC coding program, you are going to see that every coding languages will have certain catchphrases. These are the words that are intended for a particular direction or reason in the language, and you should attempt to abstain from utilizing them anyplace else. In the event that you do utilize these words in different pieces of your code, you may wind up with a blunder alert or the program not working appropriately. The watchwords that are saved for Python include:

· None

· And

· Pass

· Or

· not

· Nonlocal

· Lambda

· Is

· In

· For

- Finally

- False

- Except

- Import

- If

- Global

- From

- Break

- Assert

- Else

- Elif

- Del

- Def

- Continue

- Class

- While

- Try

- True

- Return

- Raise

- As

- Yield

- With

How to Name the Identifiers in Your Code

The next thing that we need to focus on for a moment when it comes to your code is working with the identifiers. There are a lot of different identifiers that you are able to work with, and they do come in a variety of names, including classes, variables, entities, and functions. The neat thing that happens when you go through the process of naming an identifier is that the same rules are going to apply no matter what name you have, which can make it easier for a beginner to remember the different rules that come with them.

So, let's dive into some of the rules that we need to remember when doing these identifiers. You have a lot of different options to keep in mind when you decide to name the identifiers. For example, you can rely on using all kinds of letters, whether they are lowercase or uppercase. Numbers work well, too. You will be allowed to bring in the underscore symbol any time that you would like. And any combination of these together can help you to finish up the naming that you want to do.

However, one thing to remember with the naming rules is that you should not start the name with any kind of number, and you do not want to allow any kind of space between the words that you are writing out. So, you would not want to pick out the name of 5kids, but you could call it fivekids. And five kids for a name would not work, but five_kids would be fine.

When you are working on the name for any of the identifiers that you want to create in this kind of coding language, you need to make sure that you are following the rules above, but add to this that the name you choose has to be one that you are able to remember later. You are going to need to, at some point, pull that name back up, and if you picked out one that is difficult to remember or doesn't make sense in the code that you are doing, and you can't call it back up, it is going to raise an error or another problem along the way. Outside of these rules, you will be fine naming the identifier anything that makes sense for that part of the code.

How to Handle the Control Flow with Python

The control flow in this language can be important. This control flow is there to ensure that you wrote out the code the proper way. There are some types of strings in your code that you may want to write out so that the compiler can read them the right way. But if you write out the string in the wrong manner, you are going to end up with errors in the system. We will take a look at many codes in this guidebook that follows the right control flow for this language, which can make it easier to know what you need to get done and how you can write out codes in this language.

The Python Statements

The next topic that we need to take a look at when we do some of our codings is the idea of the statements. These are going to be a simple thing to work on when it comes to Python. They are simply going to be strings of code that you are able to write out, and then you will tell the compiler to show that string on the computer string at the right time.

When you give the compiler the instructions that it needs to follow, you will find that there are going to be statements that come with it. As long as you write these statements out in the right manner, the compiler is going to be able to read them and will show the message that you have chosen on the computer screen. You are able to choose to write these statements out as long or as short as you would like, and it all is going to depend on the kind of code that you are trying to work on at the time.

Semi-colons and Indentation

When you take a gander at a portion of the other programming languages, you will see that there are a great deal of wavy sections used to orchestrate the various squares of code or to start and end the announcements. This causes you to make sure to indent the code obstructs in these dialects to make the code simpler to peruse, despite the fact that the PC will have the option to peruse the various codes without the spaces fine and dandy.

This type of coding can make it extremely hard to peruse. You will see a ton of superfluous data that is required for the PC to peruse the code, yet can make it hard on the human eye to understand this. Python utilizes an alternate method for doing this, generally to help make it simpler for the human eye to peruse what you have. You are going to need to indent the code for this to work. A case of this is:

this function definition starts another square

def add_numbers (b, c): d= b + c

as is this one

return **d**

this function definition is the start of a new-block

if it is Sunday

print (It's Wednesday!"

and this particular one is outside of this block

print ("Print this no matter what.")

In addition, there exist a lot of languages that will use a semicolon to indicate when an instruction ends.

In any case, Python will utilize line finishes to tell the PC when a guidance will end. You'll have the option to utilize a semi-colon on the off chance that you have a couple of guidelines that are on a similar line, yet this is frequently viewed as inappropriate behavior inside the language.

Letter Case

Most scripts will treat capitalized and lowercase letters the equivalent, however Python is one of the main ones that will be case touchy. This implies the lower case and capitalized letters will be dealt with distinctively in the framework. Remember also that all the saved words will utilize lower case aside from None, False, and genuine.

These rudiments are going to make it simpler to begin with Python programming. You have to set aside a touch of effort to experience the program so as to get acquainted with it. You won't have to turn into a specialist, however, getting acquainted with a portion of the content mediator and a portion of different pieces of the program can make it simpler to utilize, and you can figure out how the various catches will function even before you begin. Evaluate a couple of the models above first to enable you to begin.

Python attempts to keep things as essential as conceivable on the grounds that it comprehends that the greater part of its clients will be learners or the individuals who are sick of other complex dialects. As should be obvious here and in the accompanying sections, there are straightforward directions that you will have the option to take care of in order to get the program to work a particular way. Concentrate on these, and you can make an incredible program without very as much work.

Remarks/Comments in Python

The Importance of the Python Comments

Any time that you are writing out new code in Python, it is important to know how to work with the comments. You may find that as you are working on the various parts of your code and changing things around, you may want to add a note or name a part of the code or leave any other explanation that helps to know what that part of the code is all about. These notes are things that you and anyone else who is reading through the code will be able to see and utilize, but they are not going to affect the code. The compiler knows that comment is going on and will just skip that and go to the next part of the code that you wrote out.

Making your own comment in Python is a pretty easy process. You just need to add in the # symbol before the note that you want to write, and then the compiler knows that a note is there and that it doesn't need to read that part of the code at all. It is possible for you to go through and add in as many of these comments to the code that you are writing as you would like, and you could fill up the whole code with comments. The compiler would be able to handle this, but the best coding practice is to just add in the amount that you really need. This helps to keep things organized and ensures that you are going to have things looking nice and neat.

There are a great deal of things that you can do in Python. It is one of the most intelligent alternatives that you will keep running into when beginning programming, and since it is so natural to utilize. In this part, we will set aside some effort to examine progressively about remarks and a portion of different parts of Python so you can begin and make your codes astonishing in a matter of seconds.

In Python programming a remark is one that will begin with the # sign and after that it will proceed until you get as far as possible of the line. For instance:

There are going be just another comments

print("Hello, How are you doing?)

This would advise the PC to simply print, "Hello, how are you doing?" All remarks are disregarded in the Python mediator since it is mostly a commentary in the program to support the software engineer or other people who may utilize the code, extraordinary things about the code. They are essentially there to state what the program should do and how it will function. It is more itemized and can be useful without hindering how the code functions.

You won't have to leave a remark on each line exactly when it is required. In the event that the software engineer feels that something needs clarified better, they would place in a remark yet don't hope to see it everywhere. Python doesn't bolster any remarks that will go over a few lines, so on the off chance that you have a more drawn out remark in the program, make sense of how to separate it into various lines with the # sign before each part.

Composing and Reading

A couple of projects will show the substance you need on the screen, or they can request certain data. You may need to start the program code by telling the peruser what your program is about. Assigning it a name or a title can make things less complex, so the other coder grasps what is in the program and can pick the correct one for them.

The most ideal approach to get the correct data to show up is to demonstrate a string strict that will incorporate the "print" work. For the individuals who don't have the foggiest idea, string literals are essentially lines of content that will be encompassed by certain statements, either a solitary or twofold statement. The type of statement that you use won't make any difference that much, yet on the off chance that you utilize one type at the start of the expression, you should utilize it toward the end. So if there are twofold statements toward the start of your expression, make sure that you stay aware of the twofold statements toward the end too.

When you need the PC to show a word or expression on the screen, you would essentially have "print" and afterward the expression after it. For instance, in the event that you need to depict.

"Hi, welcome!" you would do

Print("Welcome!")

This will make it so that "Welcome" pop up on your program for others to use. The print function will take up its very own line, so you will see that in the wake of placing this in, the code will consequently put you on another line.

Probably you might want to have the guest do a specific activity, you can go with a similar sort of thought. For instance, say you need the individual to enter a particular number with the goal that they can traverse the code you would utilize the string:

second_number = input('put the second number in.')

When utilizing the input feature, you won't consequently observe it print on another line. The content will be set just after the brief. You will likewise need to change over the string into a number for the program to work. You don't have to have a particular parameter for this either. On the off chance that you do the accompanying alternative with simply the enclosures and nothing inside, you will get a similar outcome and in some cases makes it simpler.

Variables in Python

Variables are another part of the code that you will need to know about because they are so common in your code. The variables are there to help store some of the values that you place in the code, helping them to stay organized and nice. You can easily add in some of the values to the right variable simply by using the equal sign. It is even possible for you to take two values and add them to the same variables if you want, and you will see this occur in a few of the codes that we discuss through this guidebook.

Variables are very common, and you will easily see them throughout the examples that we show.

Looking for the Operators

Another part of the code that we can focus on when working in the Python language is the idea of the operators. These are simple to use, and there are going to be a lot of the codes that you try to work on that will include these operators. But even though they are pretty easy to work with, they can add to a level of power that is so important to a lot of the codes that you want. And there are a variety of operators that you are able to focus on when you write a Python code, so you have some options.

For example, you can start out with the arithmetic functions. These are good ones to work with any time that you need to do some kind of mathematics with your code. There are going to be the assignment operators that make sure a value is assigned over to the variable that you are working on. There can be comparison operators as well, which allow you to take two parts of the code, or the code and the input from the user, and then compare them to see if they are the same or not and then reacting in the way that you would like based on the code that you wrote.

As you can see, there are a ton of different parts that come with the basics of the Python code. Many of these are going to be seen in the types of codes that you are trying to write out in Python and can really help you to start writing out some of your own codes. As we go through some of the examples, as well as the practice exercises, as we go through this guidebook, you will find that these basics are going to be found in a lot of the codes that you would like to work on.

Chapter 4: Variables and Operators

The Python variables are an important thing to work with as well. A **variable**, in simple terms, is often just going to be a box that we can use to hold onto the values and other things that show up in our code. They will reserve a little bit of the memory of our code, so that we are able to utilize it later on. These are important because they allow us to pull out the values that we would like to use at a later time without issues along the way.

These variables are going to be a good topic to discuss, because they are going to be stored inside of the memory of our code. You will then be able to assign a value over to them and pull them out in the code that you would like to use. These values are going to be stored in some part of the memory of your code and will be ready to use when you need. Depending on the type of data that you will work with, the variable is going to be the part that can tell your compiler the right place to save that information to pull it out easier.

With this in mind, the first thing that we need to take a look at is how to assign a value over to the variable. To get the variable to behave in the manner that you would like, you need to make sure that a minimum of one value is assigned to it. Otherwise, you just save an empty spot in the memory. If the variable is assigned properly to some value, and sometimes more than one value based on the code you are using, then it is going to behave in the proper manner, and when you call up that variable, the right value will show up.

As you go through and work with some of the variables you have, you may find that there are three main options that are able to use. Each of these can be useful, and it is often going to depend on what kind of code you would like to create on the value that you want to put on a particular variable. The three main types of variable that you are able to choose from here will include:

- Float: This would include numbers like 3.14, etc.

- String: This is going to be like a statement where you could write out something like "Thank you for visiting my page!" or another similar phrase.

- Whole number: This would be any of the other numbers that you would use that do not have a decimal point.

When you are working with variables in your code, you need to remember that you do not need to take the time to make a declaration to save up this spot in the memory. This is automatically going to happen once you assign a value over to the variable using the equal sign (=). If you want to check that this is going to happen, just look to see that you added that equal sign is in, and everything is going to work.

Assigning a value over to your variable is pretty easy. Some examples of how you can do this in your code would include the following:

x=12 #this is an example of an integer assignment

pi=3.14 #this is an example of a floating-point assignment

customer name=John Doe #this is an example of a string assignment

There is another option that we are able to work with on this one, and one that we have brought up a few times within this section already. This is where we will assign more than one value to one for our variables. There are a few cases where we are going to write out our code and then make sure that there are two or more values that go with the exact same variable.

To make this happen, you just need to use the same kind of procedure that we were talking about before. Of course, we need to make sure that each part is attached to the variable with an equal sign. This helps the compiler know ahead of time that these values are all going to be associated with the same variable. So, you would write out something like a=b=c=1 to show the compiler that all of the variables are going to equal one. Or you could do something like 1=b=2 in order to show that there are, in this case, two values that go with one variable.

The thing that you will want to remember when you are working with these variables is that you have to assign a value in order to make the code work. These variables are also just going to be spots in your code that are going to reserve some memory for the values of your choice.

Operators

Operators are functions or symbols that indicate a specific operation. For example, the + symbol denotes addition in Mathematics and is the addition operator in Python. You will recognize many of the operators here as those used in basic Mathematics, but you will also see some that are specific to programming.

The following is a list of the Math operators in Python:

Operation Return

y + z the sum of y and z added together

y − z the difference between y and z

-y the changed sign of y

+y the identity of y

y * z the product of y and z multiplied

y / z the quotient of y divided by z

y // z the quotient of the floor division of y and z

y % z the remainder of y / z

y ** z y to the power of z

Python, just like with many programming languages, has numerous operators like arithmetic operators addition (+), subtraction (-), multiplication (*), and division (/). Some of those operators have similar functionalities in most programming languages.

Operators are divided according to their functionality and the data type of expression or output that they produce. Most operators use signs and symbols, while some use keywords. Some operators that perform uncommon or advanced data processing use functions.

Note that not adding space between operands and operators will work. However, it is best that you avoid typing expressions like that to prevent any potential syntax errors.

Arithmetic Operators

Operation	Operator	Description	Example

Addition	+	Adds numbers	>>> 1 + 1
			
			 2
			
			 >>> _

Subtraction	-	Subtracts numbers	>>> 10 - 12
			
			 -2
			
			 >>> _

Multiplication	*	Multiplies numbers	>>> 42 * 35
			
			1470
			
			>>> _

Division	/	Divides the left-hand number by the right-hand number	>>> 132 / 11
			
			12
			
			>>> _

Floor Division	//	Divides the left-hand number by the right-hand number and returns only the whole number, effectively removing any decimal value, from the quotient	>>> 10 // 3
			
			3
			
			>>> _

| Modulus | % | Performs a floor division on the left-hand number by the right-hand number and returns the remainder | >>> 133 / 11

1

>>> _ |
| Exponent | ** | Raises the left-hand number by the right-hand power | >>> 4 ** 2

16

>>> _ |

Relational Operators

Operation	Operator	Description	Example

Is Equal to	==	Returns true if left and right hand sides are equal	>>> 999 == 999
			
			True
			
			>>> _

Is Not Equal to	!=	Returns true if left and right hand sides are not equal	>>> 24 != 123
			
			True
			
			>>> _

Is Greater Than	>	Returns true if left-hand side's value is greater than the right-hand's side	>>> 554 > 64
			
			True
			
			>>> _

Is Less Than	<	Returns true if left-hand side's value is lesser than the right-hand's side	>>> 16 < 664
			
			True
			
			>>> _

Is Equal or Greater Than	>=	Returns true if left-hand side's value is greater or equal than the right-hand's side	>>> 554 >= 64
			
			True
			
			>>> 554 >= 554

			True
			>>> _

Is Equal or Less Than	<=	Returns true if left-hand side's value is lesser or equal than the right-hand's side	>>> 16 <= 664
			
			True
			
			>>> 16 <= 16
			
			True
			
			>>> _

Assignment Operator

Operation	Operator	Description	Example

Assign	=	Assigns the value of the right-hand operand to the variable on the left	>>> x = 1
			
			>>> x
			
			1

			>>> _

Add and Assign	+=	Adds the value of the left variable and the value of the right-hand operand and assign the result to the left variable	>>> x = 14
			
			>>> x
			
			14
			
			>>> x += 16
			
			>>> x
			
			30
			
			>>> _

Subtract and Assign	-=	Subtracts the value of the left variable and the value of the right-hand operand and assign the result to the left variable	>>> x = 30
			
			>>> x
			
			30
			
			>>> x -= 4
			
			>>> x

			26
			>>> _

Multiply and Assign	*=	Multiplies the value of the left variable and the value of the right-hand operand and assign the result to the left variable	>>> x = 26
			
			>>> x
			
			26
			
			>>> x *= 10
			
			>>> x
			
			260
			
			>>> _

Divide and Assign	/=	Divides the value of the left variable by the value of the right-hand operand and assign the result to the left variable	>>> x = 260
			
			>>> x
			
			260
			
			>>> x /= 13

			>>> x
			
			20
			
			>>> _

Floor Divide and Assign	//=	Performs a floor division on the value of the left variable by the value of the right-hand operand and assign the quotient as a whole number to the left variable	>>> x = 20
			
			>>> x
			
			20
			
			>>> x //= 3
			
			>>> x
			
			6
			
			>>> _

Modulus and Assign	%=	Performs a floor division on the value of the left variable by the value of the right-hand operand and assign the remainder of the	>>> x = 6
			
			>>> x
			
			6

		quotient to the left variable	>>> x %= 4
			
			>>> x
			
			2
			
			>>> _

Exponent/Raise and Assign	%=	Raises the value of the left variable by the power of the value of the right-hand operand and assign the result to the left variable	>>> x = 2
			
			>>> x
			
			2
			
			>>> x **= 3
			
			>>> x
			
			8
			
			>>> _

Logical Operators

Operation	Operator	Description	Example

Logical And	and	Returns true if both of the operands are true	>>> True and True
			
			 True
			
			 >>> _

Logical Or	or	Returns true if at least one of the operands is true	>>> True or False
			
			 True
			
			 >>> _

Logical Not	NOT	Returns the negated logical state of the operand	>>> not True
			
			 False
			
			 >>> _

Truth Table

The operator **and** will only return True if both of the operands are True. It will always return False otherwise. The operator **or** will only return False if both operands are False. Otherwise, it will always return True. The operator **not** will return False if the operand is True and will return True if the operand is False.

Below are truth tables for operator 'and' and 'or'.

Left Operand	Logical Operator	Right Operand	Result
True		True	True
True	And	False	False
False		True	False
False		False	False

Left Operand	Logical Operator	Right Operand	Result

True		True	True
True	or	False	True
False		True	True
False		False	False

Membership Operators

Operation	Operator	Description	Example

| In | In | Returns True if left operand's value is present in the value of the right operand | >>> x = "cat and dog"

>>> a = "cat"

>>> b = "dog"

>>> c = "mouse"

>>> a in x

True

>>> b in x

True

>>> c in x

False

>>> _ |

| Not In | not in | Returns true if left operand's value is not present in the value of the right operand | >>> x = "cat and dog"

>>> a = "cat"

>>> b = "dog"

>>> c = "mouse"

>>> a not in x

False

>>> b not in x

False

>>> c not in x

True

>>> _ |

Identity Operators

Operation	Operator	Description	Example

Is	is	Returns True if left operand's identity is the same with the identity of the right operand
		
		Note: If may appear that it returns True if the values of the operands are equal, but Python evaluates the identity or ID and not the values.
		
		Equal values of a single data or variable tend to receive similar IDs. Results of
			>>> x = "a"
			
			>>> id(x)
			
			34232504
			
			>>> id("a")
			
			34232504
			
			>>> x is "a"
			
			True
			
			>>> x * 2
			
			'aa'
			
			>>> x * 2 is "aa"
			
			False

		expressions may receive new IDs or overlap with existing IDs with similar values.
		
		To check the ID of variables and data, you need to use the id() keyword/function.
		
		If you want to compare if values of the operands are equal, use == operator instead.
			>>> id(x * 2)
			
			39908384
			
			>>> id("aa")
			
			39908552
			
			>>> x * 2 is 2 * x
			
			False
			
			>>> id(x * 2)
			
			39908552
			
			>>> id(2 * x)
			
			39908384
			
			>>> _

Is Not	is not	Returns True if left operand's identity is not the same with the identity of the right operand	>>> x = "a"
			>>> id(x)
			34232504
			>>> id("a")
			34232504
			>>> x is not "a"
			False
			>>> x * 2
			'aa'
			>>> x * 2 is not "aa"
			True
			>>> _

Bitwise Operators

Operation	Operator	Description	Example

Bitwise And (AND)	&	Returns 1 for bits if both operands have 1 on the same place value. Returns 0 for 0-0, 1-0, and 0-1 combinations.	>>> 0b1101 & 0b1001
			
			9
			
			>>> bin(9)
			
			'0b1001'
			
			>>> _

Bitwise Or (OR)	|	Returns 0 for bits if both operands have 0 on the same place value. Returns 1 for 1-1, 1-0, and 0-1 combinations.	>>> 0b1101 | 0b1001
			
			13
			
			>>> bin(13)
			
			'0b1101'

			>>> _

Bitwise Exclusive Or (XOR)	^	Returns 1 for bits if both operands have 0 and 1 on the same place value. Returns 0 for 1-1 and 0-0 combinations.	>>> 0b1101 ^ 0b1001
			
			4
			
			>>> bin(4)
			
			'0b100'
			
			>>> _

Bitwise Complement	~	Flips each bit and negates the value	>>> ~0b1010
			
			-11
			
			>>> bin(-11)
			
			'-0b1011'
			
			>>> _

Bitwise Left Shift	<<	Moves bits of the left operand to left. The number of	>>> 0b1010 << 2

		shifting of bits is according to the value of the right operand.	40 >>> bin(40) '0b101000' >>> _

Bitwise Left Shift	>>	Moves bits of the left operand to right. The number of shifting of bits is according to the value of the right operand.	>>>
			0b1010 >> 2
			
			2
			
			>>> bin(2)
			
			'0b10'
			
			>>> _

Below are truth tables for operator 'and', 'or', and 'xor'.

Left Operand	Logical Operator	Right Operand	**Result**
1		1	1
1	&	0	0
0		1	0
0		0	0

Left Operand	Logical Operator	Right Operand	**Result**
1		1	1
1	|	0	1
0		1	1
0		0	0

Left Operand	Logical Operator	Right Operand	**Result**
1		1	0
1	^	0	1
0		1	1
0		0	0

Chapter 5: Data Types

Now that we've discussed the basic operators that can be used in Python, we can move on to a discussion about data types. Computer programming languages have several different methods of storing and interacting with data, and these different methods of representation are the data types you'll interact with. The primary data types within Python are integers, floats, and strings. These data types are stored in Python using different data structures, such as lists, tuples, and dictionaries. We'll get into data structures after we address the topic of data types.

Integers in Python aren't different from what you were taught in math class: a whole number or a number that possess no decimal points or fractions. Numbers like 4, 9, 39, -5, and 1215 are all integers. Integers can be stored in variables just by using the assignment operator, as we have seen in Chapter 2.

Floats are numbers that possess decimal parts. This makes numbers like -2.049, 12.78, 15.1, 8.0, and 0.23 floats. The method of creating a float instance in Python is the same as declaring an integer: just choose a name for the variable and then use the assignment operator.

While we've mainly dealt with numbers so far, Python can also interpret and manipulate text data. Text data is referred to as a "string," and you can think of it as the letters that are strung together in a word or series of words. To create an instance of a string in Python, you can use either double quotes or single quotes as shown below.

string_1 = "This is a string."

string_2 = 'This is also a string.'

However, while either double or single quotes can be used, it is recommended that you use double quotes when possible. This is because there may be times you need to nest quotes within quotes. Using the traditional format of single quotes within double quotes is the encouraged standard.

Something to keep in mind when using strings is that numerical characters surrounded by quotes are treated as a string and not as a number.

The 97 here is a string

stringy = "97"

Here it is a number

numerical = 97

String Manipulation

When it comes to manipulating strings, we can combine strings the exact way we combine numbers. All you must do is insert an addition operator in between two strings to combine them. Try replicating the code below:

```python
str_1 = "Words "

str_2 = "and "

str_3 = "more words."

str_4 = str_1 + str_2 + str_3

print(str_4)
```

What you should get back is: "Words and more words."

Python provides several easy-to-use, built-in commands to alter strings. For instance, adding .upper() to a string will make all characters in the string uppercase, while using .lower() on the string will make all the characters in the string lowercase. These commands are called "functions," and we'll discuss them in greater detail later in the book. For now, know that Python has already done much of the heavy lifting for you when it comes to manipulating strings.

```python
uppercase_string = "all uppercase".upper()

print(uppercase_string)
```

What you should get back is: "ALL UPPERCASE"

String Formatting

Another method of manipulating strings include string formatting, accomplished with the "%" operator. We discussed the fact that the "%" symbol returns remainders when carrying out mathematical operations, but it has another use when working with strings. In the context of strings, the % symbol allows you to specify values/variables you would like to insert into a string and then have the string filled in with those values in specified areas. You can think of it as sorting a bunch of labeled items (the values beyond the % symbol) into bins (the holes in the string you've marked with %).

Try running this bit of code to see what happens:

string_to_print = "With the modulus operator, you can add %s, integers like %d, or even floats like %2.1f." % ("strings", 25, 12.34)

print (string_to_print)

The output of the print statement should be as follows:

"With the modulus operator, you can add strings, integers like 25, or even floats like 12.3."

The "s" modifier after the % is used to denote the placement of strings, while the "d" modifier is used to indicate the placement of integers. Finally, the "f" modifier is used to indicate the placement of floats, and the decimal notation between the "%" and "f" is used to declare how many digits need to be displayed. For instance, if the modulator is used like this %2.1, it means you need two digits before the decimal place and one digit after the decimal place displayed, hence 12.3 was printed out even though we gave 12.34.

There's another way to format strings in Python. You can use the built-in "format" function. We'll go into what functions are exactly in later chapters, but for now, we just need to understand that Python provides us with a handy shortcut to avoid having to type out the modulus operator whenever we want to format a string. Instead, we can just write something like the following:

"The string you want to format {} ".format(values you want to insert).

The braces denote the location where you want to insert the value. To insert multiple values, all you need to do is create multiple braces and then separate the values with commas. In other words, you would type something like this:

string_to_print = "With the modulus operator, you can add {0:s}, integers like {1:d}, or even floats like {2:2.2f}."

print(string_to_print.format("strings", 25, 12.34))

Inside the brackets goes the data type tag and the position of the value in the collection of values you want to place in that spot. Try shifting the numbers in the brackets above around and see how they change.

Remember that Python, unlike some other programming languages, is a zero-based system when it comes to positions, meaning that the first item in a list of items is always said to be at position zero/0 and not one/1.

One last thing to mention about string formatting in Python is that if you are using the format function and don't care to manually indicate where a value should go, you can simply leave the brackets blank. Doing so will have Python automatically fill in the brackets, in order from left to right, with the values in your list ordered from left to right (the first bracket gets the first item in the list, the second bracket gets the second item, etc.).

Type Casting

The term "type casting" refers to the act of converting data from one type to another type. As you program, you may often find out that you need to convert data between types. There are three helpful commands in Python that will allow the quick and easy conversion between data types: int(), float() and str().

All three of the above commands convert what is placed within the parenthesis to the data type outside the parentheses. This means that to convert a float into an integer, you would write the following:

int(float here)

Because integers are whole numbers, anything after the decimal point in a float is dropped when it is converted into an integer (i.e. 3.9324 becomes

3, 4.12 becomes 4). Note that you cannot convert a non-numerical string into an integer, so typing: int("convert this") would throw an error.

The float() command can convert integers or certain strings into floats. Providing either an integer or an integer in quotes (a string representation of an integer) will convert the provided value into a float. Both 5 and "5" become 5.0.

Finally, the str() function is responsible for the conversion of integers and floats to strings. Plug in any numerical value into the parenthesis and get back a string representation of it.

We've covered a fair amount of material so far. Before we go any further, let's do an exercise to make sure you understand the material we've covered thus far.

Assignment and Formatting Exercise

Here's an assignment. Write a program that does the following:

- Assigns a numerical value to a variable and changes the value in some way

- Assigns a string value to some variable

- Prints the string and then the value by using string formatting

- Converts the numerical data into a different format and prints the new data form

Give it your best shot before looking below for an example of how this can be done.

Ready to see an example of how this can be accomplished? See below:

```
R = 9

R = 9 / 3

stringy = "There will be a number following this sentence: {}".format(R)

print(stringy)

R = str(R)

print(R)
```

Chapter 6: Control Statements

Sometimes, you may need to run certain statements based on conditions. The goal in control statements is to evaluate an expression or expressions, then determine the action to perform depending on whether the expression is <u>TRUE</u> or <u>FALSE</u>. There are numerous control statements supported in Python:

If Statement

With this statement, the body of the code is only executed if the condition is true. If false, then the statements after **If block** will be executed. It is a basic conditional statement in Python.

Example:

```
#!/usr/bin/python3

ax = 7

bx = 13

if ax > bx:

    print('ax is greater than bx')
```

The above code prints nothing. We defined variables **ax** and **bx**. We then compare their values to check whether ax is greater than bx. This is false, hence nothing happens. The $\geq$ is "<u>greater than</u>" sign. Let us change it to $\geq$, this symbol means: "<u>less than sign</u>".

Let see how we can write:

```
#!/usr/bin/python3

ax = 7

bx = 13

if ax < bx:

    print('ax is greater than bx')
```

This prints the following:

```
ax is greater than bx
```

The condition/expression was true, hence the code below the **If** expression is executed. Sometimes, you may need to have the program do something even if the condition is false. This can be done with an indentation in the code.

Example:

```
#!/usr/bin/python3

ax = 10

if ax < 5:
```

```
    print ("ax is less than 5")

  print (ax)

if ax > 15:

    print ("ax is greater than 15")

  print (ax)

  print ("No condition is True!")
```

In the above code, the last **print()** statement is at the same level as the two Ifs. This means even any of the two is true, this statement will not be executed. However, the statement will be executed if both Ifs are false. Running the program outputs this:

```
No condition is True!
```

The last **print()** statement as executed as shown in the result above.

If-Else Statement

This statement helps us specify a statement to execute in case the **If** expression is false. If the expression is true, the **If**block is executed. If the expression is false, the **Else** block will run. The two blocks cannot run at the same time. It's only one of that can run. It is an advanced **If** statement.

Example:

```
#!/usr/bin/python3

ax = 10

bx = 7

if ax > 30:

        print('ax is greater than 30')

else:

        print('ax isnt greater than 30')
```

The code will give this result once executed:

```
ax isnt greater than 30
```

The value of variable **ax** is 30. The expression **if ax > 30:** evaluates into a false. As a result, the statement below **If**, that is, the first **print()** statement isn't executed. The else part, which is always executed when the **If** expression is false will be executed, that is, the **print()** statement below the **else** part.

Suppose we had this:

```
#!/usr/bin/python3

ax = 10
```

```
bx = 7
```

```
if ax < 30:

        print('ax is less than 30')

else:

        print('ax is greater than 30')
```

This will give this once executed:

```
ax is less than 30
```

In the above case, the **print()** statement within the **If** block was executed. The reason is that the **If** expression as true.

Another example:

```
#!/usr/bin/python3
```

```
ax = 35
```

```
if ax % 2 ==0:

        print("It is eve")

else:

        print("It is odd")
```

The code outputs:

```
It is odd
```

The **If** expression was false, so the else part was executed.

If Elif Else Statement

This statement helps us test numerous conditions. The block of statements under the **elif** statement that evaluates to true is executed immediately. You must begin with **If** statement, followed by **elif** statements that you need, and lastly the **else** statement, which must only be one.

Example:

```
#!/usr/bin/python3

ax = 6

bx = 9

bz = 11

if ax > bx:

        print('ax is greater than bx')
```

elif ax < bz:

> print(**'ax is less than bz'**)

else:

> print(**'The else part ran'**)

The code outputs the following:

```
ax is less than bz
```

We have three variables namely **ax, bx,** and **bz.** The first expression of the If statement is to check whether ax is greater than bx, which is false. The **elif** expression checks whether **ax** is less than **bx,** which is true. The **print()** statement below this was executed.

Suppose we had this:

#!/usr/bin/python3

ax = 6

bx = 9

bz = 11

if ax > bx:

```
    print('ax is greater than bx')
```

```
elif ax > bz:
```

```
    print('ax is less than bz')
```

```
else:
```

```
    print('The else part ran')
```

The code will output:

```
The else part ran
```

In the above cases, both the **If** and **elif** expressions are false, hence the **else** part was executed.

Another example:

```
#!/usr/bin/python3
```

```
day = "friday"
```

```
if day == "monday":
```

```
    print("Day is monday")
```

```
elif day == "tuesday":
```

```python
        print("Day is tuesday")

elif day == "wednesday":

        print("Day is wednesday")

elif day == "thursday":

        print("Day is thursday")

elif day == "friday":

        print("Day is friday")

elif day == "saturday":

        print("Day is saturday")

elif day == "sunday":

        print("Day is sunday")

else:

        print("Day is unkown")
```

The value of **day** if **friday**. We have used multiple **elif** expressions to check for its value. The **elif** expression for **friday** will evaluate to true, hence its **print()** statement will be executed.

Nested If

An **If** statement can be written inside another **If** statement. That is how we get nested **If**.

 Example:

```
#!/usr/bin/python3

day = "holiday"

balance = 110000

if day == "holiday":

  if balance > 70000:

        print("Go for outing")

 else:

        print("Stay indoors")

 else:

        print("Go to work")
```

We have two variables **day** and **balance**. The code gives the following result:

```
Go for outing
```

The first **if** expression is true as it's a holiday. The second **if** expression is also true since balance is greater than 70000. The **print()** statement below that expression is executed. The execution of the program stops there. Suppose the balance is less than 70000 as shown below:

#!/usr/bin/python3

day = "holiday"

balance = 50000

if day == "holiday":

  if balance > 70000:

        print(**"Go for outing"**)

  else:

        print(**"Stay indoors"**)

else:

      print(**"Go to work"**)

The value of **balance** is <u>50000</u>. The first **if** expression is true, but the second one is false. The nested else part is executed. We get this result from the code:

```
Stay indoors
```

Note that the nested part will only be executed if and only if the first **if** expression is true. If the first **if** is false, then the un-nested **else** part will run. Example:

```
#!/usr/bin/python3

day = "workday"

balance = 50000

if day == "holiday":

  if balance > 70000:

        print("Go for outing")

  else:

        print("Stay indoors")

else:

        print("Go to work")
```

The value for **day** is **workday**. The first **if** expression testing whether it's a holiday is false, hence the Python interpreter will move to execute the un-nested **else** part and skip the entire nested part. The code gives this result:

```
Go to work
```

Chapter 7: Loops and Functions

Loops

The ability to make decisions is a critical component of most computer programs. Another is the ability to repeat or loop the program through a specific set of tasks.

All programs, other than those that perform a specific task and exit, contain at least one loop. Typically, this is the main loop, where the program continually loops, waiting for user or object input for it to act upon.

Additionally, loops can be used to apply repetitive processes on objects using a compact set of instructions.

Python offers two types of loops.

The **for** loop and the **while** loop.

They both allow for the repetitive looping through a specific operation but differ in how they test if the loop should continue to be processed.

For Loop

In the **for** loop, the loop will execute over a given range of items.

For example:

```
>>> for x in range(0,3):
print(x)
0
1
2
```

There are several things to note in this example.

First off, the syntax is similar to the **if** statements we covered earlier.

The **for** loop is ended with a colon.

With a single instruction in the **for** loop, we can leave that instruction on the same line immediately after the colon. A return after that will indent to the next instruction outside the **for** a loop.

If the for command contains multiple instructions, start those instructions on the next line. They will be indented to show they are contained within the loop.

A blank line entered at the end will close out the loop and drop the indent down from the loop for the next instructions outside the loop.

Range Command

Next, we have the **range()** command.

The range command is a built-in python method used to generate a range of numbers and is not explicitly part of the for loop syntax.

It is just there to make the numbers to iterate through. Like other ranges in python, the numbers provided do not represent a range from 0 – 3. They represent outputting three numbers starting at 0, which gives us 0, 1, and 2.

3 is not output in the range.

This is slightly different than the for loops you might be accustomed to in other languages. In those, a given range generally included the last number defined – for x=1 to 10, for example, would output 1 – 10, not one through 9.

While we use the range() function to generate the numbers to iterate over in the for loop, it is by no means the only option.

We can pull numerical values from any iterable source to iterate over that source.

For example, we can use the length of lists, tuples, or strings to process through that item.

```
>>> x=['apples', 'oranges', 'bananas', 'peaches', 'plums']
>>> for y in x:
print(y)

apples
oranges
bananas
```

peaches

plums

It is important to note, in this case, that we are iterating sequentially through the list values and setting y equal to those.

We are not setting y to the position values of 0 through 4.

If we had used print(x[y]) - or print the string at the position y in the list - we would get an exception stating that y cannot be str.

To iterate through a list using the position number, we would have to set y to a numeric range and iterate through it that way.

```
>>> for y in range(0, len(x)):
print(x[y])
```

apples

oranges

bananas

peaches

plums

Going this route makes it easier to get every x value within the list.

The range method includes a step value attribute that allows us to step through the list in spaces other than 1.

For example, to get every other item in our list we would use:

```
>>> for y in range(0, len(x), 2):
print(x[y])
```

apples

bananas

plums

Or, get the list backwards:

```
>>> for y in range(len(x)-1, -1, -1):
print(x[y])
```

plums

peaches

bananas

oranges

apples

While Loop

The **while** loop continues while a specified condition is true.

For example:

```
>>> y=1
>>> while y<=10:
print(y)
y+=1
```

```
1
2
3
4
5
6
7
8
9
10
```

In this case, the loop will continue as long as y is less than or equal to 10.

Unlike **for** loop, which is specified to execute over a prespecified range and then exit, the while loop will continue as long as the specified condition is true; therefore, while loops can become infinite loops or code that loops forever.

To prevent that, code must be included within the loop that will make the condition false at some point.

In this case, $y +\!=1$ increments y by one each time the loop executes. When y becomes 11, the conditional becomes false, and the loop ends.

If you make a mistake and your program gets stuck in an infinity loop, you can exit the program by pressing ctrl-c.

Break Command

There is one additional way of gracefully exiting a **for** or **while** loop.

The **break** command forces the loop to terminate prematurely.

When coupled with an **if** statement, break can be used to conditionally and exit a loop early.

In most cases, choosing which loop structure to use and properly designing the code within the loop will negate the need for the break statement, so it is generally considered better if you can avoid it.

There are some cases, however, where it can be necessary.

Functions, Classes, and Methods

We learned how to branch programs through conditional statements and how to repeat through a set of instructions with loops efficiently. The next level of sophistication to explore is the function.

A **function** is a block of code that performs a specific, repetitive task that can be compartmentalized and called by another piece of code.

Our first code example in this book looked at a small program that calculated the volume of a cylinder.

This is an excellent example of something that should be written as a function. It is a clearly defined task that will never change.

By placing the code in a function, we can write it once and call it as many times as we need without rewriting it within the program.

Additionally, we can pull that code from one program and use it in any program we want, provided we call it properly.

This write-once/use everywhere property is a key benefit to object-oriented programming tools like Python. It saves time not just in development but in debugging and deployment as well because the code only has to be written and debugged once.

Our original program for calculating the volume of a cylinder looked like this:

```python
# import math

import math

# assign variables
r=5 # radius
h=10 # height
V=0 # volume

# calculate volume of a cylinder
V=(math.pi*math.pow(r,2))*h # volume=(π*r^2)*h

# output the result
print(V)
```

If we had a much bigger program in which we wanted to calculate the volume of various cylinders, we could copy and paste this where necessary within the program, and it would work fine.

The better way to handle that is to convert this to a function.

Ideally, well-written functions would be completely self-sufficient. By that, I mean they should rely only on local variables (no globals).

Any values they need to function should be passed from outside, and any results they produce should be returned to the calling source.

So, in this case, we will need to set up our function to accept the radius, height as parameters. From the provided parameters, we can calculate the volume and return that value to the calling code.

The structural syntax for a Python function makes this easy. The basic format is as follows:

```
Def functionName(arg1, arg2,..):
code to run
return return-value
```

The function name can be anything that is not a reserved word or reference already in use by the program.

arg1, arg2, … are variables that can accept values from the calling code.

These parameters will be local variables to the function and follow the same rules as any variable in Python.

Functions do not require these parameters, but they will be used in most cases.

Code to run is any python code which is necessary for the function to perform its task.

The return command at the end will send the value of whatever variable you specify back to the calling code.

The return call is also not required but will be used in most cases.

So to convert our volume of a circle calculation to a function, it will look like this:

```
# import math

import math

# define function
def cylinderVol(r, h): # r=radius, h=height
V=(math.pi*math.pow(r,2))*h # volume=(π*r^2)*h

return V # return the volume

# output the result

print(cylinderVol(5, 10)) # print the volume of a cylinder r=5, h=10
```

So, what we did was take the repetitive code necessary for the actual calculation and put it in a function which we named 'cylinderVol'.

That function accepts two arguments – r for the radius and h for the height. Those two arguments are all that is needed to complete the calculation.

We then do that calculation and place the result in V, which is then returned to the caller.

Instead of simply calling the function from a **print()** statement, we could have assigned a variable to the call like this:

vol = cylinderVol(5,10)

vol would then be equal to 785.3981633974483 – or the returned value of the function.

Because this function relies only on the values it is passed by the caller, it is entirely portable and can be used in any program provided it is called in the same fashion. This fact allows us to build into the next level, which is the class.

A **class** is typically defined as a group of related functions.

We currently have the code established to calculate the volume of a circle. We could expand upon that to create a volume class that would include functions for calculating the volume of cylinders and cubes.

import math

import math

define class

class Volume(object):
def cylinderVol(self, r, h): # r=radius, h=height

```python
self.V=(math.pi*math.pow(r,2))*h # volume=(π*r^2)*h
return self.V

def cubeVol(self, l, w, h):
self.V=(l*w*h)
return self.V

# output the result

vI=Volume() #create an instance of the Volume class

V=vI.cylinderVol(5,10) #set V by calling cylinderVol in the volume class

print(V) #print the result

V=vI.cubeVol(5,10,10) #set V by calling cylinderVol in the volume class

print(V) #print the result
```

In this example, we create a class called Volume.

Within it, we define two methods - in a class, the functions are called methods – one for cylinderVol and one for cubeVol.

These take the same arguments we used for the corresponding freestanding functions with one exception. The first argument of self.

In object-oriented programming, the value of self is commonly used to refer to the instance of the object created by the class.

In our code above, we first create an instance of the class by assigning a variable to it (vI=Volume()).

The self term is used to access the class-specific values then assigned to the vI variable instance.

This allows different instances to have different values for the same variables, and it allows us to test those values.

A clearer example may be that if we were creating a racing game, we could have a car class. That class could have methods for assigning make, model, speed, color, or other variables to a 'car' object.

If we created two cars by calling carA=car() and carB=Car() then carA's self property will point to a different car object than the self-property of carB.

Those two objects can store different values for the variables defined in the class for make, model, speed, and color.

Once the object vI is created, we can call its' methods in the same fashion we called our function earlier.

The only difference is we call a method using dot syntax (V=vI.cylinderVol(5,10)). By doing so, we call the method specific to that object and therefore utilize any special properties that are unique to that instance.

To improve usability and portability, Python allows us to save files like this separately and import them into other files as a whole.

We can create a file called volumemath.py and include in it a whole series of classes and methods designed to handle whatever volume calculations we would like to address.

That file can be saved separately and imported into our python projects on an as-needed basis.

Python allows defining the main function.

The following code is used to define and execute that function.

```
def main():

# main code

if __name__ == "__main__":
main()
```

The whitespace between the def main(): and the start of the main code is required. Failure to include it will throw an exception.

The second statement is an if..then that ensures the code is only called from the main file.

If you always use that code and mistakenly include it in a module or library, then the main() will not be called because the __name__ property will be set to the module name, not main.

Since python executes the file starting at the beginning as soon as it loads, these should be called early in your main file.

While a main() function is not required, it offers several advantages over not using one.

First, as a function, all the variables used in main() will be local to main().

Without the main() function declaration, all the variables will be global. That is also the case for all variables declared outside any functions in the main file.

Finally, this allows the main function to be called safely from a loaded module. Loading the main function from a module will allow more options in debugging.

Infinite Loop

You should always be aware of the greatest problem with coding loops: infinity loops. Infinity loops are loops that never stop. And since they never stop, they can easily make your program unresponsive, crash, or hog all your computer's resources. Here is an example similar to the previous one but without the counter and the usage of a break.

>>> while (True):

print("This will never end until you close the program")

This will never end until you close the program

This will never end until you close the program

This will never end until you close the program

Whenever possible, always include a counter and break statement in your loops. Doing this will prevent your program from having infinite loops.

Continue

The continue keyword is like a soft version of break. Instead of breaking out from the whole loop, "continue" just breaks away from one loop and directly goes back to the loop statement. For example: >>> password = "secret"

>>> userInput = ""

>>> while (userInput != password):

userInput = input()

continue

print("This will not get printed.")

Wrongpassword

Test

secret

>>> _

When this example was used on the break keyword, the program only asks for user input once regardless of anything you enter, and it ends the loop if you enter anything. This version, on the other hand, will persist in asking for input until you put the right password. However, it will always skip on the print statement and always go back directly to the while statement.

Here is a practical application to make it easier to know the purpose of the continue statement.

```
>>> carBrands = ["Toyota", "Volvo", "Mitsubishi", "Volkswagen"]

>>> for brands in carBrands:

if (brands == "Volvo"):

continue

print("I have a " + brands)

I have a Toyota

I have a Mitsubishi

I have a Volkswagen

>>> _
```

When you are parsing or looping a sequence, there are items that you do not want to process. You can skip the ones you do not want to process by using a continue statement. In the above example, the program did not print "I have a Volvo" because it hit ***continue*** when a Volvo was selected. This caused it to go back and process the next car brand on the list.

Syntax of a Function

The syntax of a function looks like this:

```
def function_name(parameters):

"""docstring"""

statement(s)

return [expression]
```

Here is a breakdown of what the syntax of a function:

def keyword: This marks the beginning of the function header.

function_name: This is a unique name that identifies the function. The rules of the function name are almost similar to those of a variable we learned at the beginning of this book.

parameters or **arguments**: Values are passed to the function by enclosing them in parentheses (). Parameters are optional.

The colon marks the end of the function header.

"""docstring""": (Docstring) is an optional documentation string. It describes the purpose of the function.

statement(s): There must be one or more valid statements that make up the body of the function. Notice that the statements are indented (typically tab or four spaces).

There may be an optional return statement that returns a value or values from the function.

Creating and calling a function

To use a function you create in your script, you will need to call it from the Python prompt, program, or function.

Exercise55: Creating a function

```
def greeting(name):

"""This function greets the user when

the person's name is passed in as

a parameter"""

print ("Greetings,", name + "!")
```

You can call a function by simply typing its name along with the appropriate parameters.

Modify the previous Exercise55 code to see how you can call the function greeting.

Exercise56: Calling a function

```
def greeting(name):

"""This function greets the user when

the person's name is passed in as

a parameter"""

print ("Greetings,", name + "!")

    username = str(input("Enter your name: "))

greeting(username)
```

The code in Exercise55 first defines a function called a greeting, which requires one argument, name. It will prompt the user to enter a string, which will be assigned the variable username and used as the argument when the function greeting is called.

Docstring

The first string of text immediately after the function header is called the documentation string, or in short, docstring. This section of the function is optional and briefly explains what the function does. It is a good practice to include a descriptive docstring whenever you create a new function because you, or another programmer going through your code at a later time, may need it to understand what the function does. Always document your code!

We have exhaustively explained what our greeting function does. As you can see, we used a triple quote string to make it possible for the description to extend to multiple lines. Within the attribute of the function, the docstring is available as ___*doc*___.

For instance, the greeting function would appear in the Python shell print() function output as in Exercise57.

Printing the docstring

```
def greeting(name):

"""This function greets the user when

the person's name is passed in as
```

an argument."""

print ("Greetings,", name + "!")

    print (greeting.__doc__)

The return statements

The optional return statement in a function is used as an exit to return execution back to where it was called. The syntax of the return statement as we have seen takes this form:

return [expression_list]

The return statement may contain expressions that get evaluated to return a value. If there is no expression in the statement or when the **return** statement is not included in the function, the defined function will return a **None** object when called. Our greeting function in Exercises 55 through 57 returns a value of **None** because we have not included a return statement.

The return statement

def agegroup_checker(age):

```python
"""This function returns the

user's age group name based

on the age entered."""

if age >= 18:

agegroup = "Adult"

elif age >= 13:

agegroup = "Teenager"

elif age >=0:

agegroup = "Child"

else:

agegroup = "Invalid"

return (agegroup)

age = int(input("Enter your age to check age group:"))

print ("Your age group is:", agegroup_checker(age))
```

Function Arguments

In Python, you can call a function using any of these four types of formal arguments:

- Default arguments.

- Required arguments

- Keyword arguments

- Variable-length arguments

Default arguments

A default argument assumes the default value if no value is specified within the function's call parameters.

Default arguments

```
def studentinfo(name, gender = "Male"):

"This function prints info passed in the function parameters."

print ("Name:", name)

print ("Gender:", gender)

return;

studentinfo ( name = "John")

studentinfo ( name = "Mary", gender = "Female")
```

In Exercise59, you can see how we have specified the default value for the parameter gender as "Male". When we do not define the gender within one of the values, the default value is used.

Required arguments

Required arguments must be passed to the function in the exact positional order to match the function definition. If the arguments are not passed in the right order, or if the arguments passed are more or less than the number defined in the function, a syntax error will be encountered.

Keyword arguments

Functions calls are related to keyword arguments. This means that when a keyword argument is used in a function call, the caller should identify the argument by the parameter name. With these arguments, you can place arguments out of order or even skip them entirely because the Python interpreter will be able to match the values provided with the keywords provided.

Keyword arguments

def studentinfo(name, age):

"This function prints info passed in the function parameters."

```
print ("Name:", name, "Age:", age)

return;

studentinfo (age = 21, name = "John")
```

Note that with keyword arguments in Exercise60, the order of the parameters does not matter.

Variable-length arguments

In some cases, a function may need to process more arguments than the number you specified when you defined it. These variables are known as variable-length arguments. Unlike required and default arguments, variable-length arguments can be included in the definition of the function without being assigned a name.

The syntax for a function with non-keyword variable-length arguments takes this format:

```
def studentinfo(name, age):

"This function prints info passed in the function parameters."

print ("Name:", name, "Age:", age)

return;
```

```
studentinfo (age = 21, name = "John")
```

Notice that an asterisk is placed right before the tuple name that holds the values of non-keyword variable arguments. If no additional arguments are defined when the function is called, the tuple will remain empty.

Chapter 8: Objects and Concepts

In this chapter, we will introduce the concepts of object-oriented programming and see some simple examples.

Objects

While in procedural programming functions (or procedures) are the main organizational element in object programming (also known as OOP, or Object-Oriented Programming), the main organizational element is the objects.

In procedural programming, data and functions are separated, and this can create a number of problems, including:

- data and functions must be managed separately;

- you need to import the functions you want to use;

- you need to switch the data to the functions;

- it is necessary to verify that the data and functions are compatible;

- it is more difficult to extend and modify functionality;

- the code is harder to maintain;

- it's easier to introduce bugs.

In object programming, objects have the function of enclosing both data and behavior in a single organizational unit. This has several advantages:

- data and functions are grouped together;

- it is easy to know what operations can be performed on the data;

- You do not need to import functions to perform these operations;

- there is no need to switch data to functions;

- functions are compatible with the data;

- it's easier to extend and modify functionality;

- the code is easier to maintain;

- it's harder to introduce bugs.

Let's see a simple example: we have the base and height of 100 different rectangles, and we want to know the area and perimeter of each rectangle. Using a procedural approach, we can solve the problem by creating two separate functions that accept base and height:

```
>>> # we define two functions to calculate area and perimeter
>>> def calc_rectangle_area(base, height):
...     """Calculate and return the area of a rectangle."""
...     return base * height
...
>>> def calc_rectangle_perimeter(base, height):
...     """Calculate and return the perimeter of a rectangle."""
...     return (base + height) * 2
...
```

We can then create a list of random tuples (base, height), iterate it with a for, and pass the values to the functions:

```
>>> from random import randrange
>>> # create a list of 100 tuples (base, height) with random values
>>> rects = [(randrange(100), randrange(100)) for x in range(100)]
>>> rects
[(16, 39), (92, 96), (60, 72), (99, 32), (39, 5), (43, 6), (51, 28), ...]
>>> # we iterate the list of rectangles then print out
>>> # base, height, area, perimeter of each rectangle
>>> for base, height in rects:
...     print('Rect:', base, height)
...     print(' Area:', calc_rectangle_area(base, height))
...     print(' Perimeter:', calc_rectangle_perimeter(base, height))
...
Rect: 16 39
  Area: 624
  Perimeter: 110
Rect: 92 96
  Area: 8832
  Perimeter: 376
Rect: 60 72
  Area: 4320
  Perimeter: 264
...
```

Using object-oriented programming, we can instead create a class that represents the rectangle object. Instead of representing rectangles as a list of tuples, we use the class to create 100 <u>instances</u> of the Rectangle class,

```
>>> # define a class representing a generic rectangle
>>> class Rectangle:
...     def __init__(self, base, height):
...         """Initialize the base and height attributes."""
...         self.base = base
...         self.height = height
...     def calc_area(self):
...         """Calculate and return the area of the rectangle."""
...         return self.base * self.height
...     def calc_perimeter(self):
...         """Calculate and return the perimeter of a rectangle."""
...         return (self.base + self.height) * 2
...
```

and instead of calling the functions passing the base and height, we call the instance methods:

```
>>> # create an instance of the Rectangle class with base 3 and height 5
>>> myrect = Rectangle(3, 5)
>>> myrect.base  # instance has a base
3
>>> myrect.height  # instance has a height
5
>>> myrect.calc_area()  # it is possible to calculate the area directly
15
>>> myrect.calc_perimeter()  # and also the perimeter
16
```

As we can see in the next example, creating and using instances is quite intuitive:

Now that we have a basic idea of how classes work, we can create the 100 rectangles and calculate the area and perimeter:

```
>>> from random import randrange
>>> # create a list of 100 instances of Rectangle with random values
>>> rects = [Rectangle(randrange(100), randrange(100)) for x in
range(100)]
>>> # we iterate the list of rectangles and print out
>>> # base, height, area, perimeter of each rectangle
>>> for rect in rects:
...     print('Rect:', rect.base, rect.height)
...     print(' Area:', rect.calc_area())
...     print(' Perimeter:', rect.calc_perimeter())
...
Rect: 78 44
 Area: 3432
 Perimeter: 244
Rect: 0 85
 Area: 0
 Perimeter: 170
Rect: 32 2
 Area: 64
 Perimeter: 68
```

As we can see by comparing the two examples, using object programming we can work directly with single objects (the instances of Rectangle). The list no longer contains tuples but rectangles, and to calculate area and perimeter it is no longer necessary to pass the base and height explicitly. Also, calc_area() and calc_perimeter() are associated with the instance, so you don't need to import functions, you don't risk to use the wrong function (for example, a function that calculates the area of a triangle), you don't risk to pass the base or the height of the wrong rectangle or passing them in the wrong order.

Terms and Concepts

In the above examples, we have introduced some new terms and concepts that are commonly used in object programming.

Classes

Classes are used to define the characteristics of an object, its <u>attributes</u> (e.g. base and height) and its <u>methods</u> (e.g. calc_area() and calc_perimeter()). Classes are "abstract" - they don't refer to any specific object, but they represent a model that can be used to create <u>instances</u>. For example, the Rectangle class specifies that rectangles have a base, a height, an area, and a perimeter, but the class does not refer to any particular rectangle.

Instances

Instances are objects created from a class. For example, Rectangle(3, 5) returns an instance of the Rectangle class that refers to a specific rectangle that has base 3 and height 5. A class can be used to create different instances of the same type but with different attributes, like the 100 different rectangles we saw in the previous example. You can use the methods defined by the class with each instance by simply making instance.method() (e.g. myrect.calc_area()).

Attributes

Attributes are values associated with the instance, such as the base and height of the rectangle. The attributes of each instance are separate: each instance of Rectangle has a different base and height. To access an attribute just make instance.attribute (e.g. myrect.base).

Methods

Methods describe the behavior of the object, they are similar to the functions and are specific to each class. For example, both the Rectangle class and the Triangle class can define a method called calc_area(), which will return different results depending on the type of the instance. Methods can access other attributes and methods of the instance: this allows us, for example, to call myrect.calc_area() without having to pass the base and height explicitly. To call a method just make instance.method() (e.g. myrect.calc_area()).

Inheritance

Another important concept in programming is inheritance. Inheritance allows us to create a new class from an existing class and extend or modify it.

For example, you can create a Square class that inherits from the Rectangle class. Since the 4 sides of a square have the same length, it is no longer necessary to require base and height separately, so in the Square class, we can change the initialization to require the length of a single side. In this way, we can define a new class that instead of accepting and defining the two base and height attributes defines and accepts a single side attribute. Since the square is a particular type of rectangle, the methods to calculate area and perimeter work without changes, and we can then use calc_area(), and calc_perimeter() inherited automatically from the class Rectangle without having to redefine them.

It is also possible to define hierarchies of classes, for example, you can define the class Husky that inherits from the class Dog that inherits from the class Mammal that inherits from the class Animal. Each of these classes can define attributes and behaviors common to all objects of that class, and the subclasses can add new ones.

Python also supports multiple inheritances: you can define new classes that inherit methods and attributes from several other classes by combining them.

Superclasses and Subclasses

If the Square class inherits from the Rectangle class, we can say that Rectangle is the superclass (or base class), while Square is the subclass. The operation of creating a subclass from an existing class is sometimes called a subclassing.

Operator Overloading

In Python, classes also allow us to redefine operator behavior: this is called operator overloading. You can define special methods that are called automatically when an operator is used with an instance of the class.

For example, we can define that myrect1 < myrect2 returns True when the area of myrect1 is lower than that of myrect2, or we can define that myrect1 + myrect2 returns a new instance of Rectangle created by the combination of myrect1 and myrect2.

When to Use Object Programming

Although object programming is a very useful and powerful tool, it is not the solution to all problems. Often creating a simple function is sufficient, and it is not necessary to define a class.

In general, object-based programming can be the right solution if:

- the class we want to create represents an object (e.g. Rectangle, Person, Student, Window, Widget, Connection, etc.);

- we want to associate both data and behavior to the object;

- we want to create different instances of the same class;

Object-based programming may not be the best solution if:

- the class we want to create does not represent an object, but for example a verb (e.g. Find, Connect, etc.);

- we just want to represent data (better to use a data structure like list, dict, namedtuple, etc.) or just behaviors (better to use functions, possibly grouped in a separate module);

- we want to create only one instance of the same class (better to use a module to group data and functions).

Of course, there are also exceptions (e.g., the singleton pattern, which defines a class with only one instance). Python is a multiparadigm language, so it is important to choose the paradigm that best suits the situation.

Chapter 9: Tips to Learn Python Programming

Before we end some of the work that we are doing with Python, it is time to really dive into some of the tips and tricks that you are able to use when it is time to improve your own skills in Python.

When learning a new coding language, you may find that it is easier to work with a language if you have some tips and skills to make it happen. But it does still take some time to really learn the language and get it ready for the work that you want to accomplish.

Some of the codings that we did throughout this guidebook are meant to make things easier and will ensure that we are able to see some of the results that we want in the process as well.

With this said, let's take a look at some of the simple tips that you are able to use in order to improve your own Python skills and ensure that you will be able to get some of that code writing done in no time.

Try Our Many Approaches

As a programmer, it is important to realize that there are going to be a lot of different approaches that you are able to use when it comes to working in the Python language, and with some of the other aspects of Python as well.

It is easy as a beginner to think that you have to work with just one approach and then stick with it the whole time, but doing this is just going to lead to frustration during the process because it won't end up working the way that you would like.

As you work through some of the codings that you would like to accomplish with Python, why not consider trying out more than one approach to the coding process. While it may be seen as typical to employ the same coding techniques that are general throughout the whole application, this is not always going to be the best method for you to use.

Instead of working in this manner, don't be scared to try a little bit of experimentation to see whether or not one technique is going to be better or more optimal in a situation compared to another one. This will help to keep you sharp and innovative in some of the different coding approaches that you use, no matter what language you would like to work with.

It encourages you to think more outside of the box, which makes it easier to apply new coding techniques in order to obtain some results that are much faster in your own coding applications.

Keep the Code Light and Small

As with anything, the smaller and lighter that you can keep the code, the better. Yes, there may be a way to do some of the codings that you would like that is bulky and takes a lot of lines of code to accomplish. But the more lines of code that you have for a program, no matter what program you are working with, the harder it is to get this to run. Sometimes there isn't a way to get around all of this. But it can definitely speed up some of the work that you do and how well the program works if you are able to keep the code to a minimum and ensure that it is not going to get too heavy and bogged down in the process.

When you are working in programming, no matter which programming language you choose to work with, it is often the case that the simplest is going to be the fastest.

And since you have to make sure that your application or program is able to keep up with the fast-paced world of those who are going to use it, it is very important that the code you try to write out in Python turns out to be as compact and easy to use as possible.

Any time that we can compact some of the code that we are using and make it easier to work with, we are going to reduce the amount of latency that is found and can speed things up. As you go through the development of any of your programs, you have to be ready to ask some of the tough questions to figure out whether something is actually necessary or not.

Figure out whether one of the frameworks or the modules you are using is actually necessary for the work that you are doing and if there is an easier way to write the same kind of code instead.

Avoid Loops That Are Not Needed

We spent some time earlier talking about the loops and why these are so important to some of the code that we want to write. But if we spend too much time working on loops when they are not needed, rather than focusing on some of the other great coding options that you are able to work with, then it can become a big problem.

The consensus of most experts is that if you add in too much looping in any programming language is going to be a bad thing. It can often add too much strain on the server that you are working with.

Spend Time Coding Daily

When you are learning any new coding language that you want to focus on, consistency is going to be one of the most important factors that you need to spend your time on.

It is best to make a commitment to code a bit each day. This is not something that you have to spend hours on each day, and in fact, this is actually a bad thing, but a few minutes on a daily basis will help us to learn how to do the coding a bit better and will ensure that we are going to get the results that we would like.

Make it your goal to practice coding with Python about 20 to 25 minutes a day. This is not that much time for you to try out a few different methods that we talk about in this guidebook and more. You can always add in some more coding time as needed, but you also have the chance to work for a bit and make sure that you are able to learn how to do some of the different parts.

Write it All Out

As you start to progress on the journey of coding as a new programmer, you may run across the idea of needing to take notes about the things that you are doing. The truth is, yes, you should! There is a lot of research out there that suggests how taking notes by hand is actually going to be one of the most beneficial things that you can do to ensure you retain the information you want for the long term.

This is going to be even more beneficial to those who are not coding just for fun but who is in this with the idea of working towards a goal of being a full-time developer in the future.

Once you are ready to handle some of the smaller programs and projects with Python, writing by hand can also help you to plan out your code before you decide to work with the coding on the computer. For a lot of new programmers, it is much easier for them to write out things, and it will save them a lot of time when they are ready to actually work on some of the codings.

Take Some Breaks

When we are learning how to do some programming with Python, we have to remember that no matter how much we get into the process, we have to take a break on occasion. It is common for those who are brand new to the process to keep on working, and this can make it frustrating when something isn't going the right way, and can really make us feel overwhelmed in the process as well. It is also best if you are able to take some study breaks on a regular basis to ensure that you can absorb some of the information and not feel like you are too tired in the process.

One technique that you may want to work with here is known as the Pomodoro Technique. This is an idea where you work hard for 35 minutes, trying to get as much done as possible at that time, and then you take a short break.

This break maybe about five minutes, but you close the computer or walk away and give your body a break from it. Then you repeat the process two or three more times. After those times, you take a longer break, maybe 30 minutes this time. The idea with this one is that you get away from work and can give your mind a break, making you more efficient and helping you to not get weighed down by all of the work.

Breaks are going to be really important no matter what kind of process you are working with, but you will find that this becomes even more important when you are doing anything like debugging your program. If you have hit a snag in your coding and you are not able to figure out what is not working and what is causing the problems, then it is time to take a break.

This is often the last thing that you want to do, but stepping away from the computer, going out for a walk, and just taking a break can be one of the best things that you can do to fix the program

Surround Yourself with Others Who Are Learning

Another thing that we need to consider doing when it comes to working with the Python program and all of the cool things that we are able to do with this language is making sure that we surround ourselves with other learners as well. This can give you some of the motivation that you need to ensure the process goes smoothly, allows you to ask questions, and helps each person in that group really have a chance to learn something new.

Though it often feels like coding is going to be an activity that we are able to do on our own, it is actually going to work the best when we are able to work with other people, rather than on our own. It is so important that when you are learning a bit about the coding process in Python that you take your time to surround yourself with other people who are in the process of learning as well.

This is going to allow you to share some of the tricks and tips that you have along the way.

Don't let this worry you if you are looking at this suggestion, and you don't know anyone else who is trying to learn how to code right now. There are a lot of options that you are able to go with when you get stuck here. There are options for meeting lots of other programmers who are passionate about learning Python as well, you just need to do a little search online in order to find these individuals.

Work with Pair Programming

The next thing that we need to take a look at is known as pair programming. This is going to be a kind of technique that will have two developers who are working at the same workstation work together in order to finish a task.

The two developers are going to be able to switch back and forth between being either the driver or the navigator.

The driver is going to be the programmer who is responsible for writing out the code. Then we have the navigator who is going to help guide the problem solving and will be able to review any of the code as it is written.

You will need to switch these two programmers back and forth in order to get the benefits and to ensure that each is able to learn along the way.

There are a lot of benefits that come with pair programming. It is going to provide you with a chance to not only have someone to review your code, but it is also going to show us how someone else may think about a problem.

Being exposed to a lot of ideas and different ways of thinking will help you in problem-solving when you go back to doing some of the codings on your own again.

Make Sure To Ask the Good Questions

While there is a lot of thought out there that there isn't such a thing as a bad question, it is important that you are careful about the questions that you are asking in programming. It is possible for you to ask a question badly, and this is going to just lead to more confusion and frustration when you do some of your own coding in the process.

When you are trying to get someone else to help you out, and if they do not have much context on the problem that you would like to solve, you will need to ask some good questions. Following the acronym below is going to ensure that you are asking the right kind of questions that can get you the help that you need:

G: Give the context on what you would like to get the code to do. Make sure that you actually describe the problem at hand as clearly as possible.

O: Outline some of the things that you have already been able to try in terms of fixing the issue.

O: Offer your best guess at what you think the problem is. This is going to help the other person know what you are thinking about this process but ensures that you have actually done a little bit of thinking about the problem at hand as well.

D: demo what is happening. You may want to include the code, the error message that comes with it, and then an outline of the steps that you have already tried that didn't fix the error or result in the error.

This is going to help the person out because they won't have to go through all of the steps to figure out what you did.

You can imagine that asking these good questions is really going to save a lot of time. If you skip out on these steps, it is really going to result in a lot of back and forth conversation between you and the person who is trying to provide you with some of the help that you need.

Working with the Python coding language can be a great experience for a lot of programmers. But having some of the tips that are above will ensure that even as a beginner, you are able to take this to the next level and actually see some of the results that you want. Make sure to check out some of the tips that you need to follow to make sure that you are able to get the most out of your Python programming overall.

Conclusion

As a beginner to programming, we want to congratulate you on making it through the first steps of this wonderful journey. Now, with your feet past the threshold, we invite you to take a look at the world beyond and really let your imagination go wild. There is no limit to what you can do once you've put your mind to it.

In this book, you have been given the basics of programming using Python. This book does not require any programming prerequisites. On the contrary, this book is designed to provide total beginners with the right tools to start programming using the Python language. Once you get to know it, Python is very easy to learn and is one of the most satisfying languages in terms of writing programs.

You have suffered through a multitude of syntax errors, exceptions, and potential system crashes. Errors are easy to identify and fix, and there is plenty of help to be had along the way, unlike many other computer programming languages that kick up errors without really telling you why or telling you what is wrong.

And now your eyes have been opened to the world of programming. So, where do you go from here?

The answer is simple: Go wherever the wind takes you.

The next step is to take your learning further. There are plenty of tutorials on the Internet and lots of courses that you can sign up for. There are also a lot of forums where a friendly and helpful community is ready to help you solve any problems you may have and help you to get ahead in programming. The most important thing is to practice; things are changing all the time in Python and, if you don't keep up with it, you will find you have to start over again.

At this point, you should know what it is that you want to do with your newly acquired programming skills. As the magician that you now are, you have to forge your own path and decide how to best utilize your magic. For instance, most of the Python authors' work involves using Application Program Interfaces (APIs). This means that the need to gather and process data is never-ending.

When it comes to yourself, there is nothing that can be better offered than information about what is out there for you to explore. There are many disciplines that are in need of your programming abilities. These few may help you choose which way you need to go.

Data scientists are in need of Python developers, as it is an extremely good tool that offers many modules to solve a lot of limitations found in other languages. However, the most important thing is how well Python developers are paid.

Machine learning is best practiced in Python, although there are other programming languages that have libraries to support it. None come close to Python, though. It is being used by corporations like Google, along with thousands of programmers around the world.

Web development using Python and Django makes it very easy to build web applications. If your passion lies there, you can do in mere minutes what it would take other developers to do in hours.

Whatever your choice, wherever the journey may take you from here, just know that you are ready to take on all the challenges you may face. We truly believe that you are armed with some of the best informational bullets we can give you and enough tips and tricks to get you started in this world of codes. As with everything else in life, view this as an adventure, and don't be afraid to venture forth and explore new territories. There is still so much more that Python can offer, and for the programmer in you looking for more advanced techniques and tips, the world is your oyster.

So go, Young Programmer, and show the world what you can do!

www.ingramcontent.com/pod-product-compliance
Lightning Source LLC
La Vergne TN
LVHW051246050326
832903LV00028B/2609